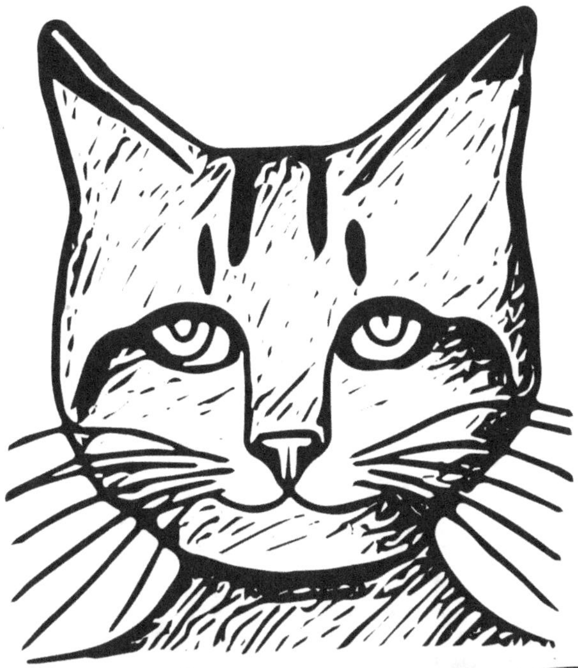

CATS

THE COLORING BOOK

CincyPet Media, LLC
PO Box 428686
Cincinnati, OH 45242

www.cincypetmag.com

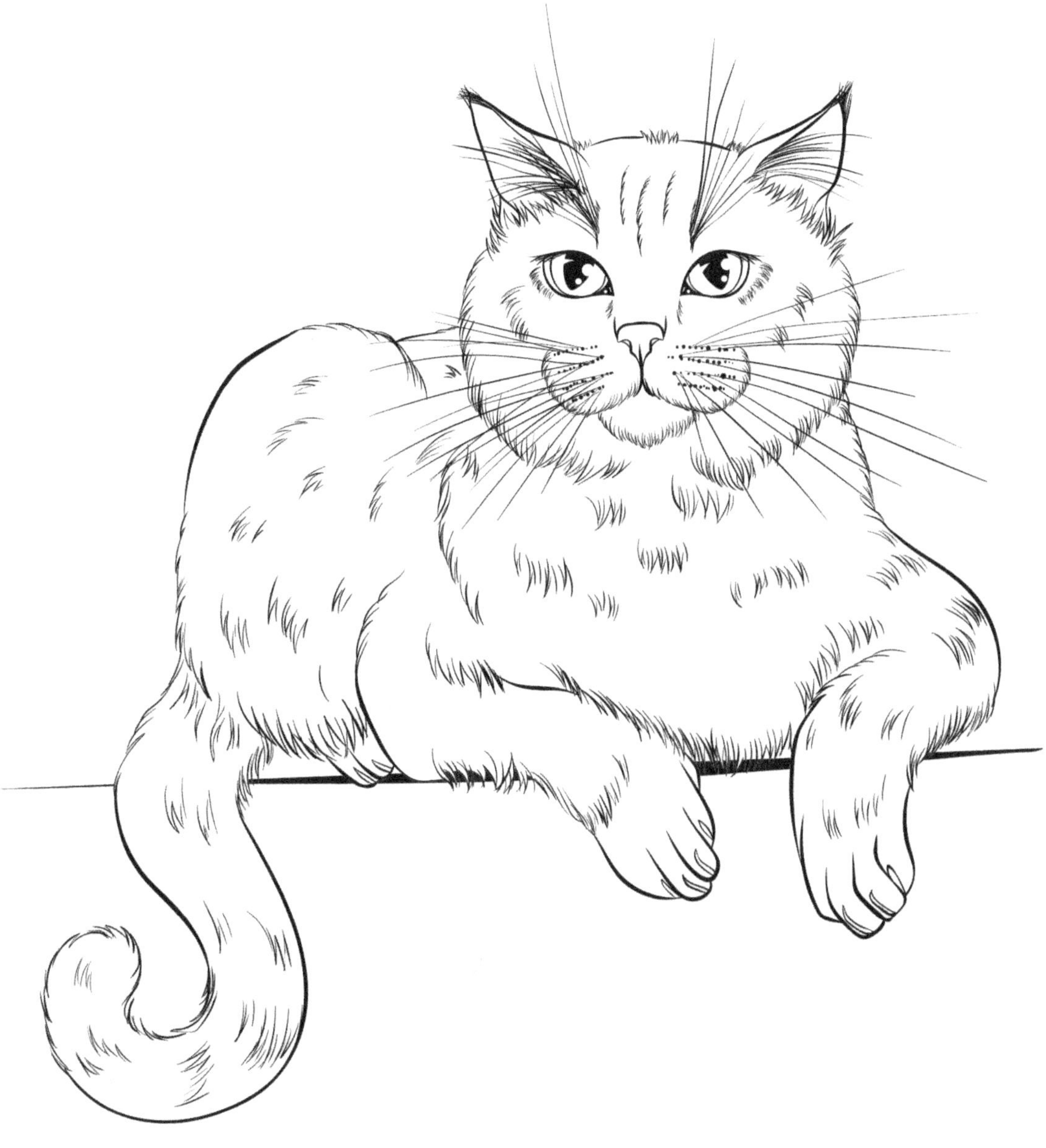

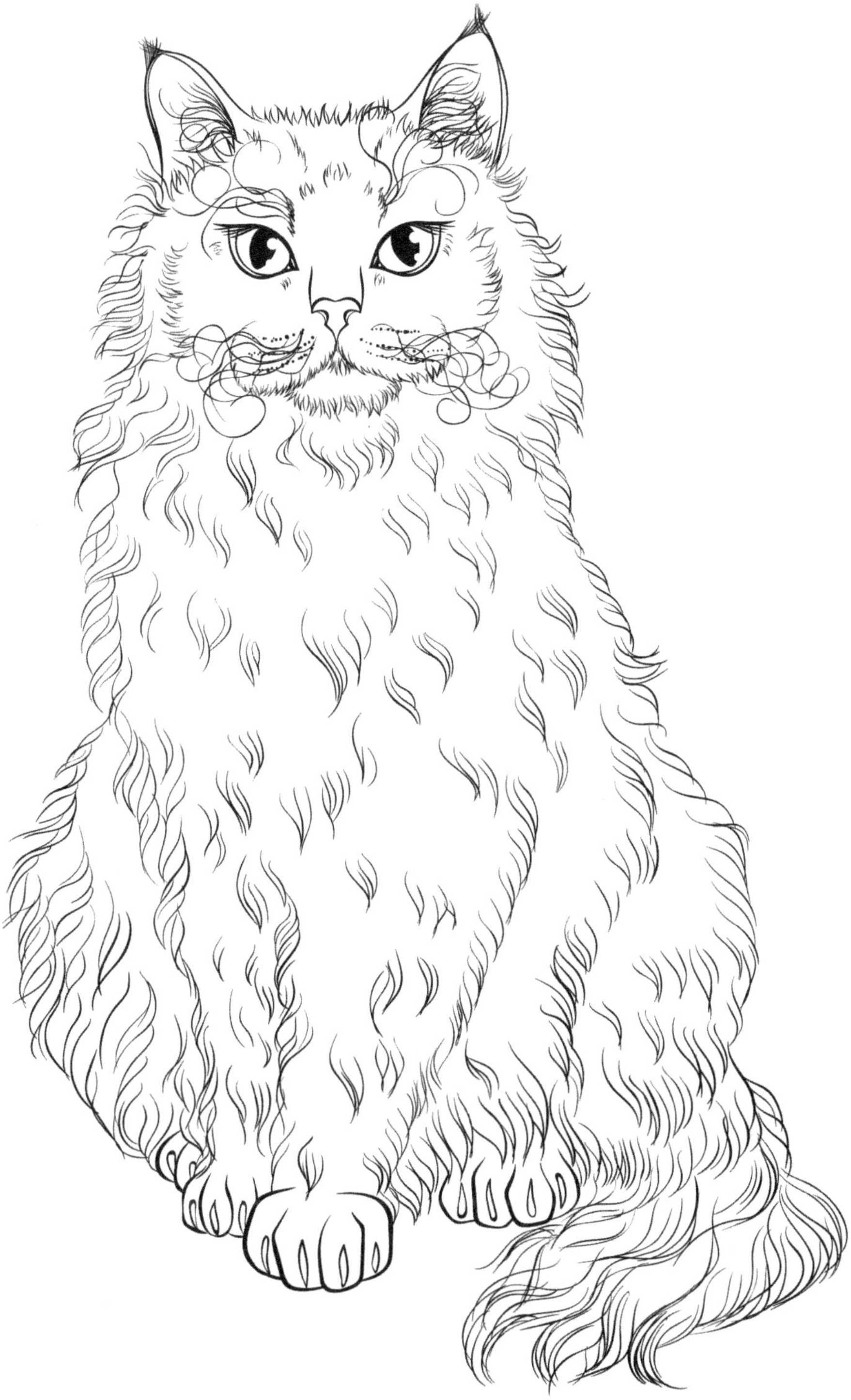

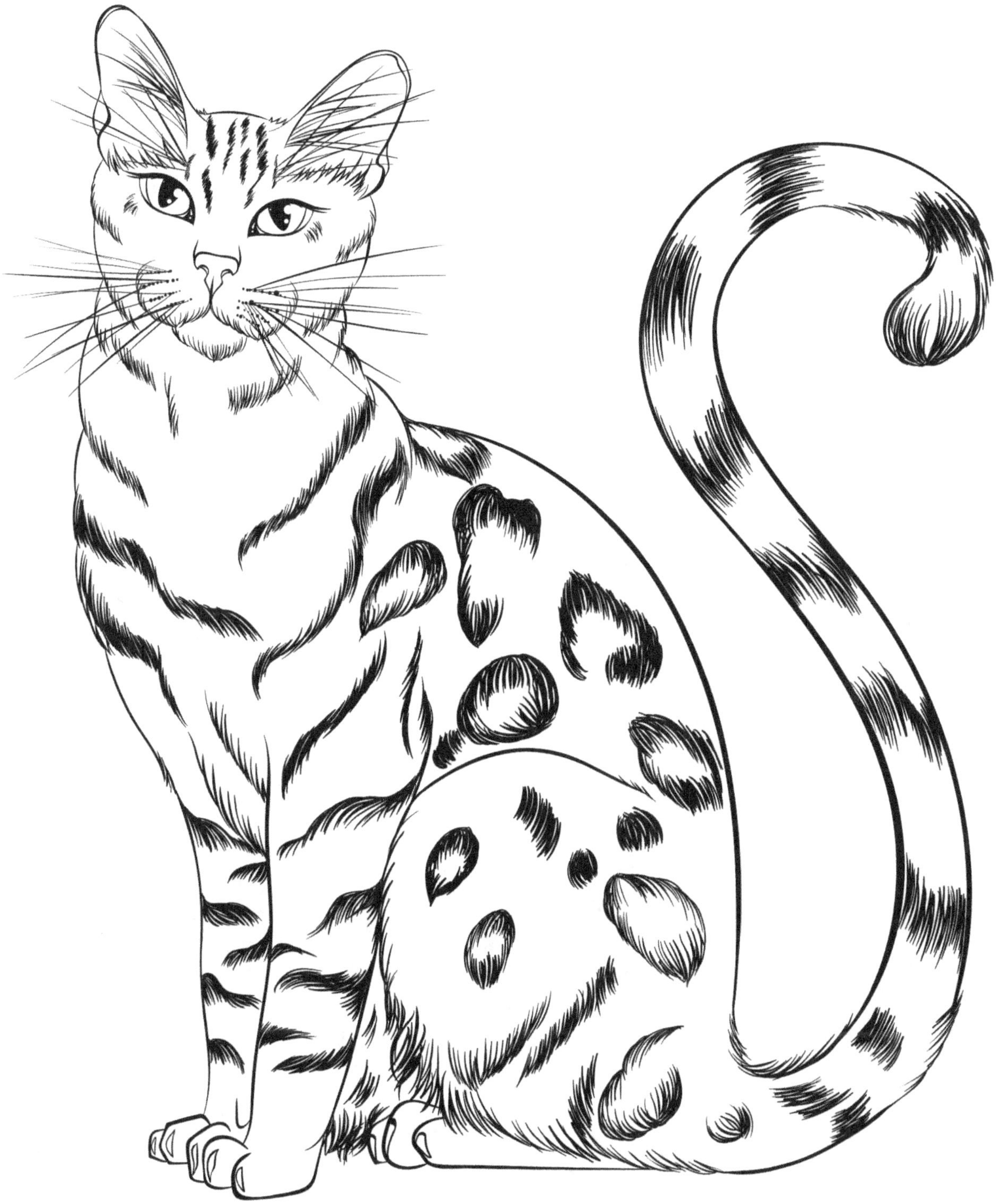

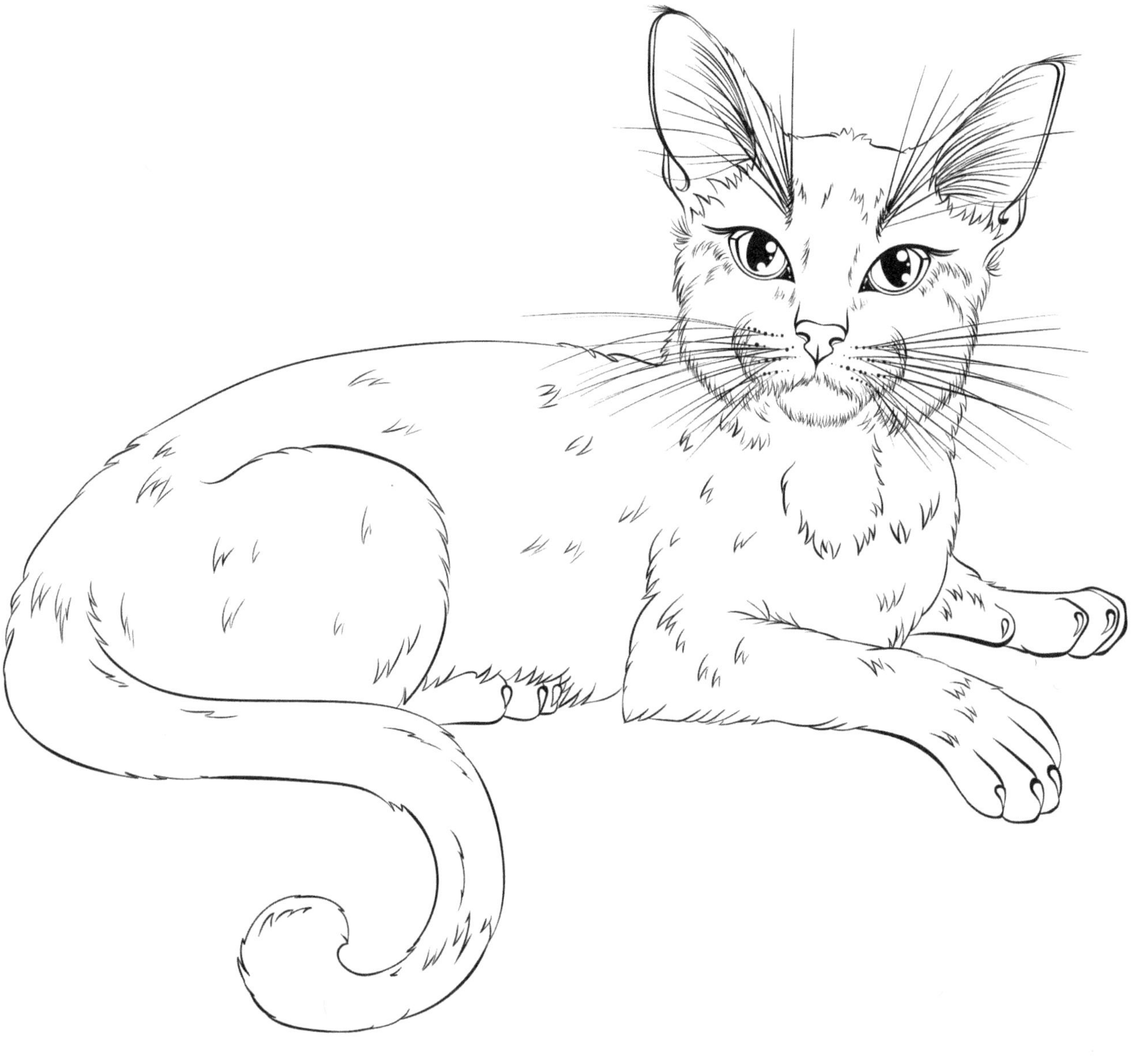

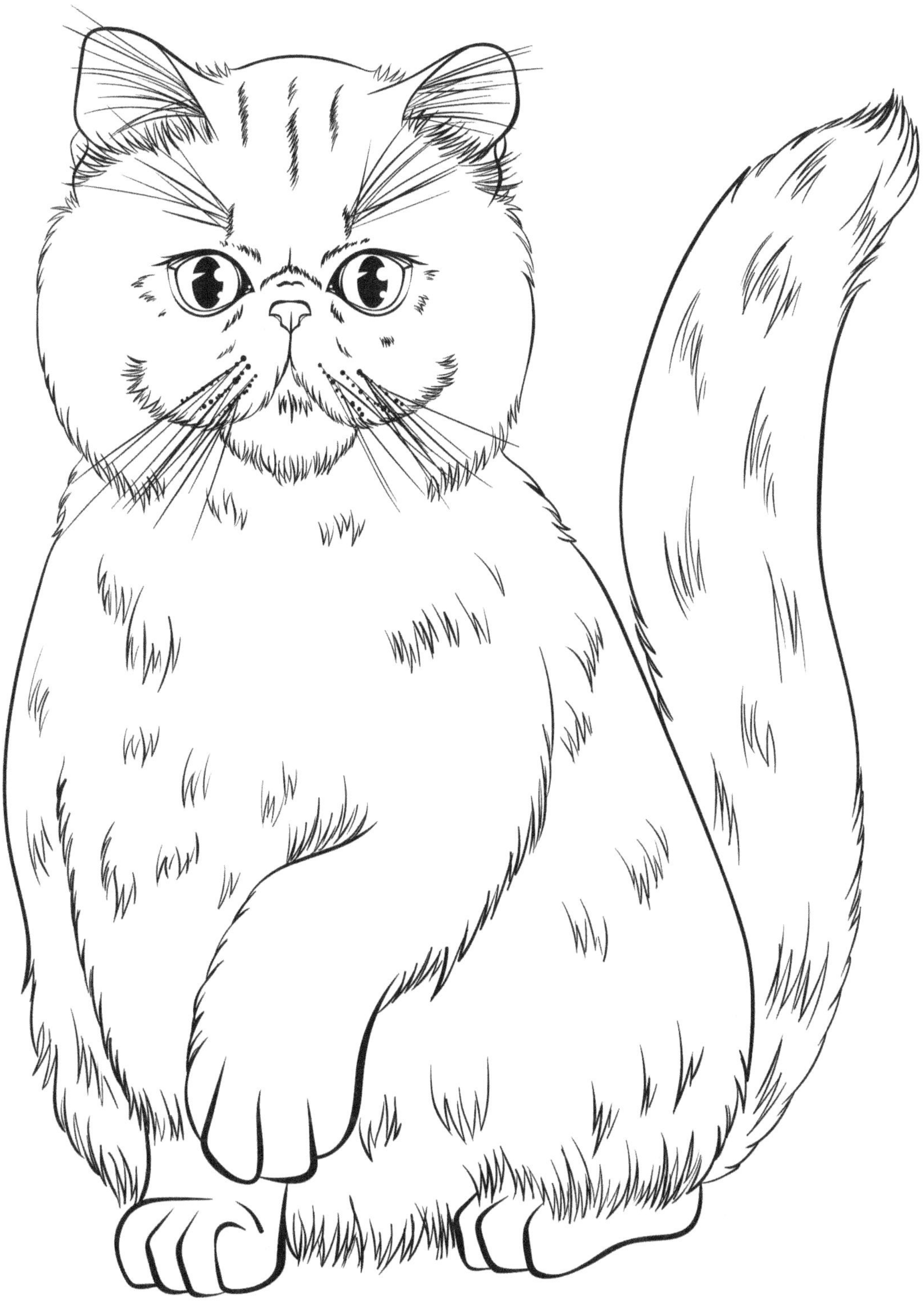

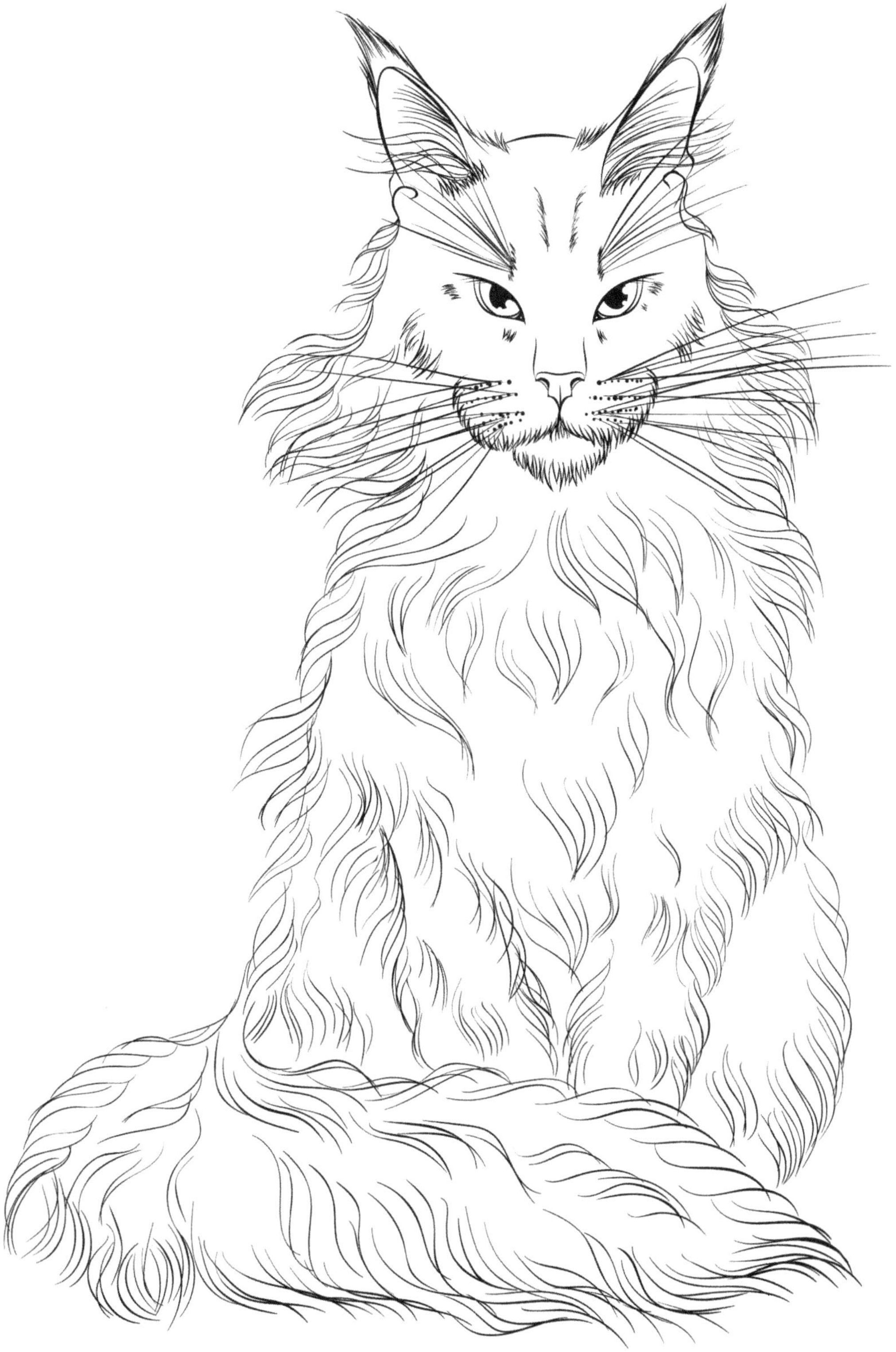

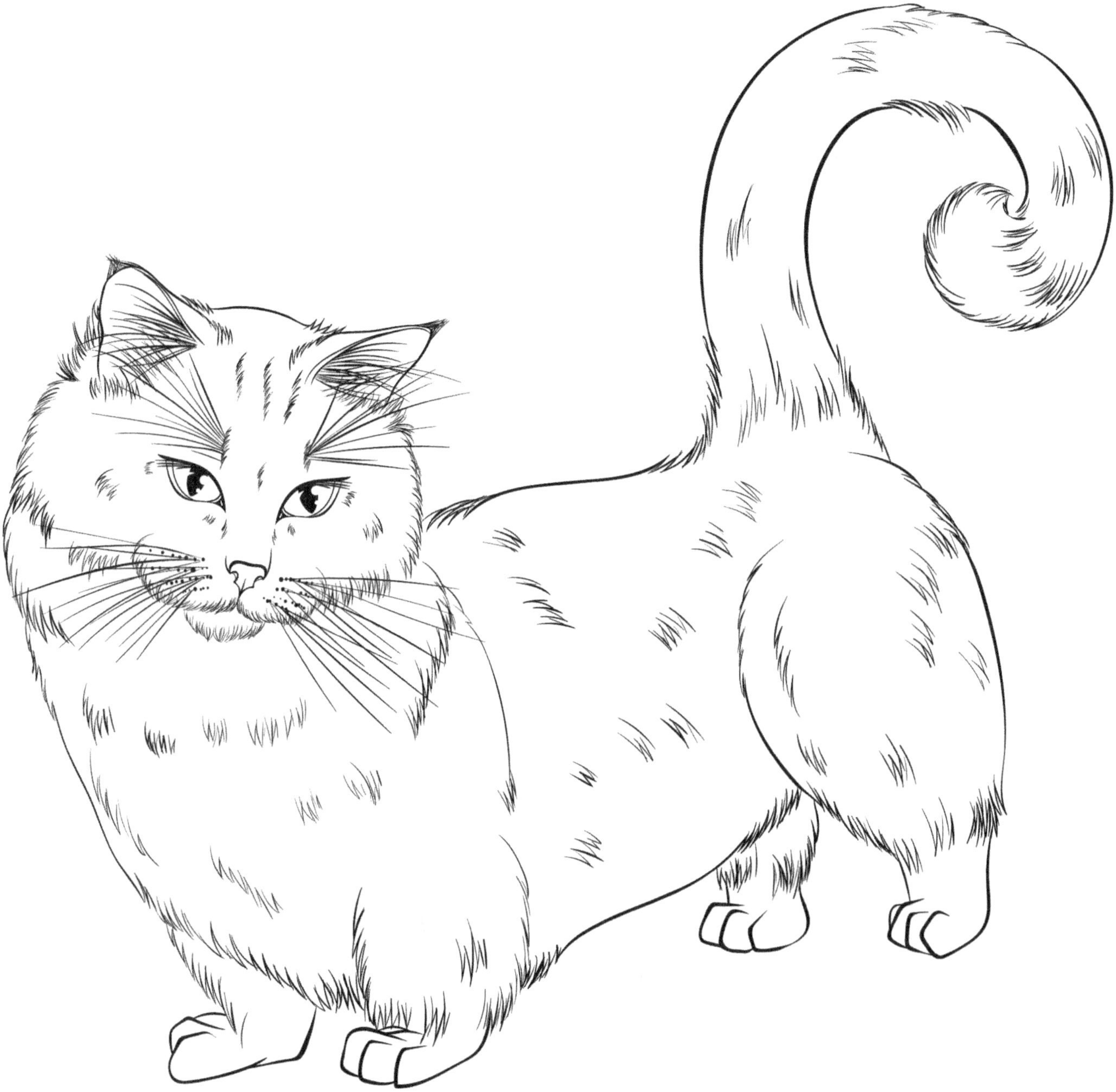

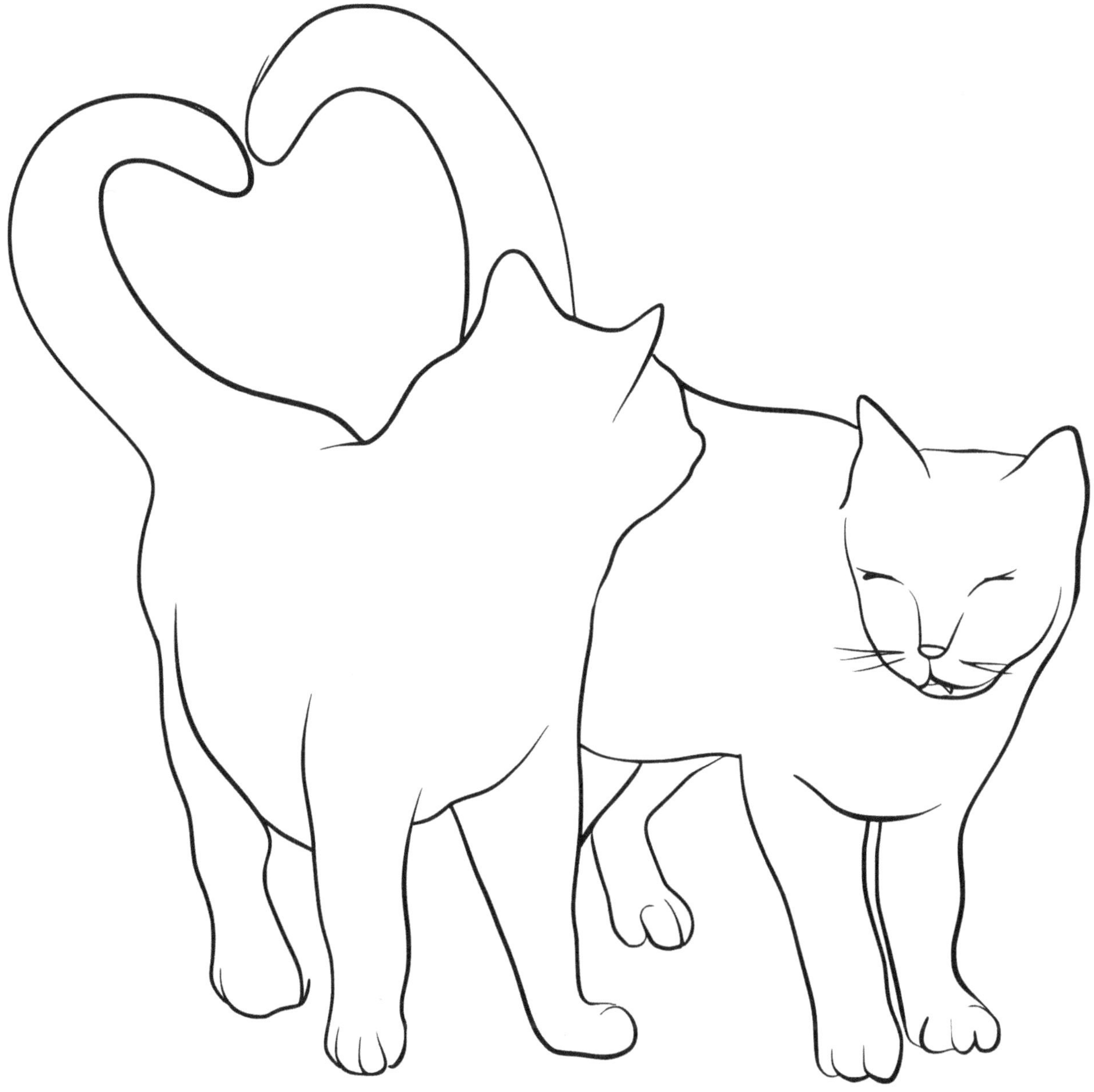

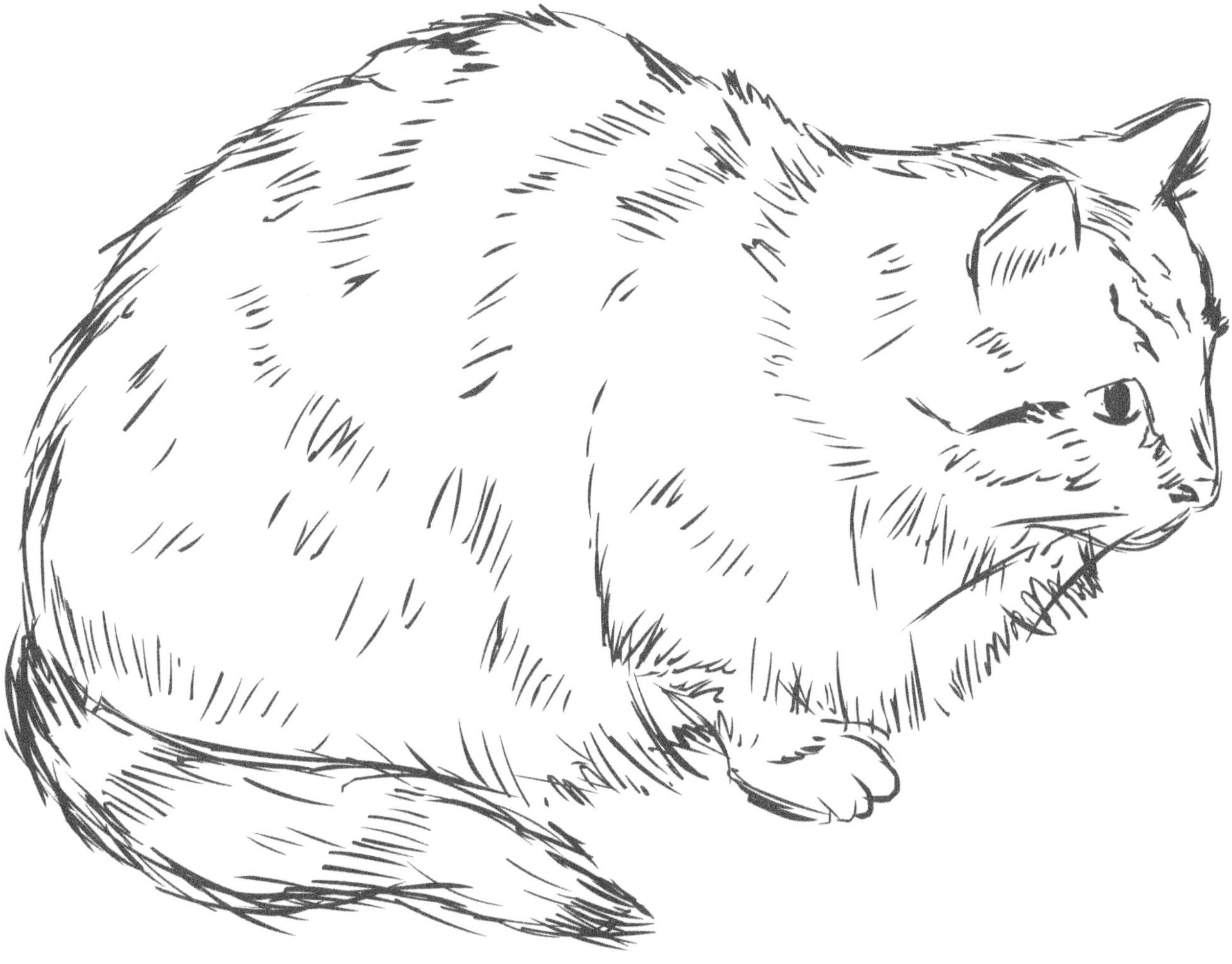

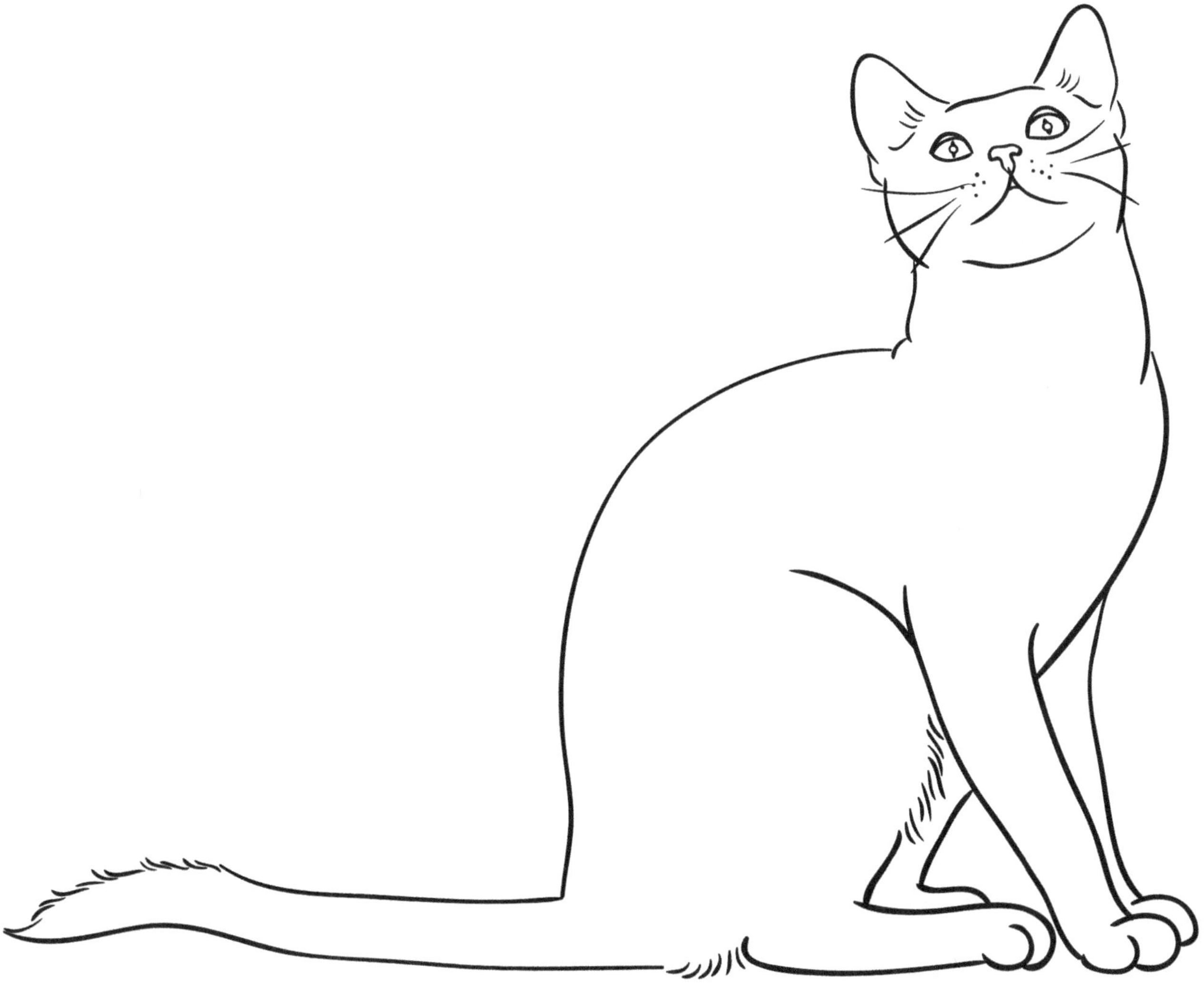

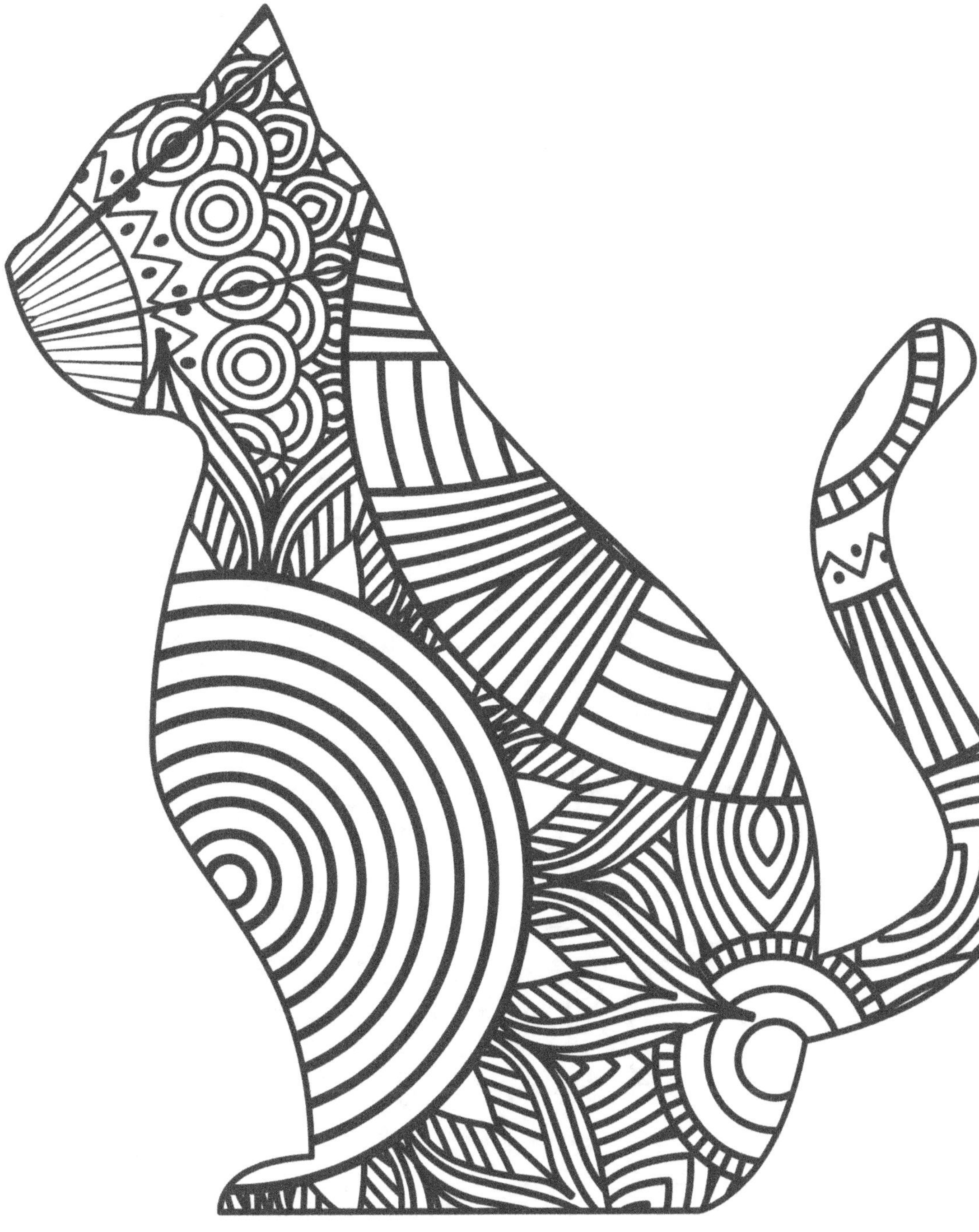

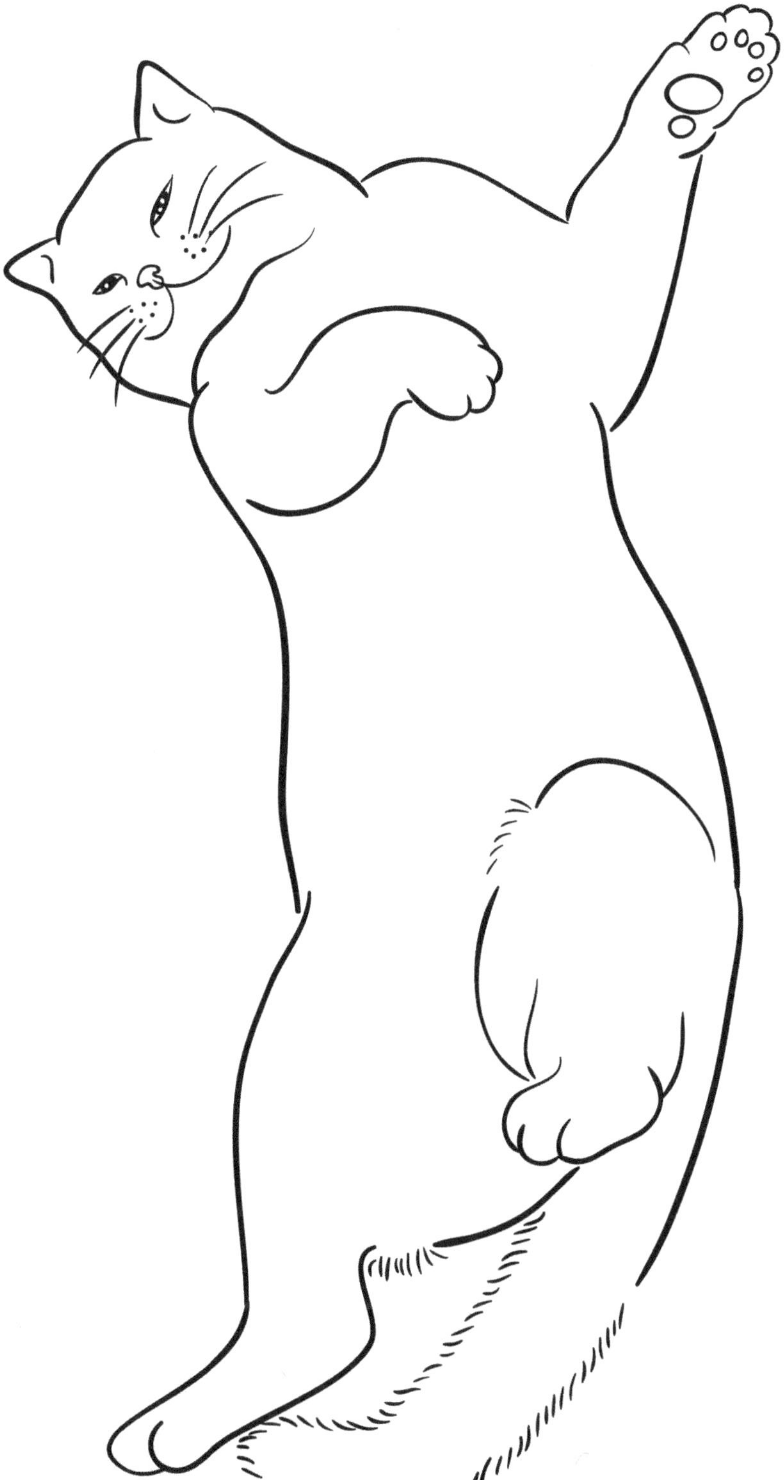

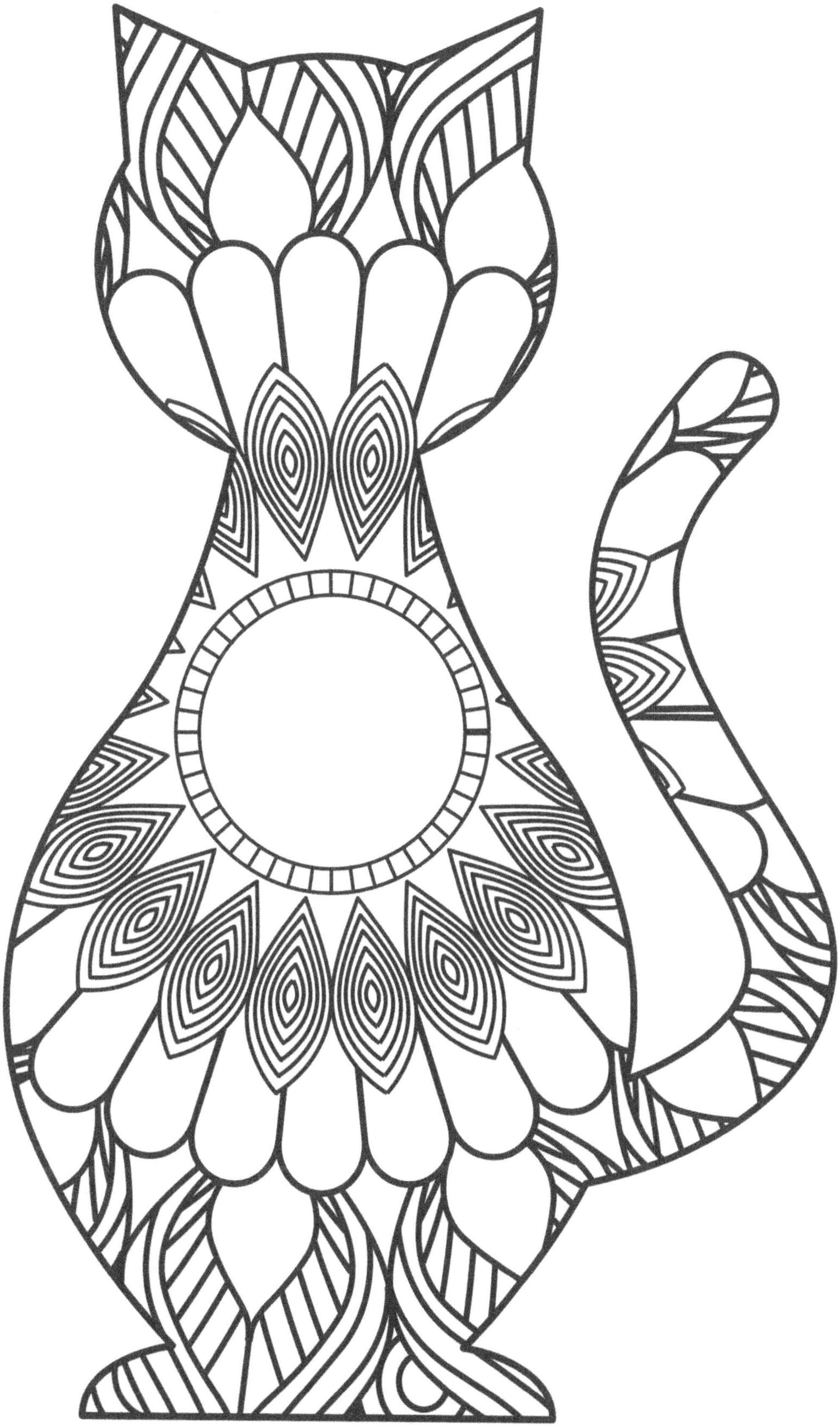

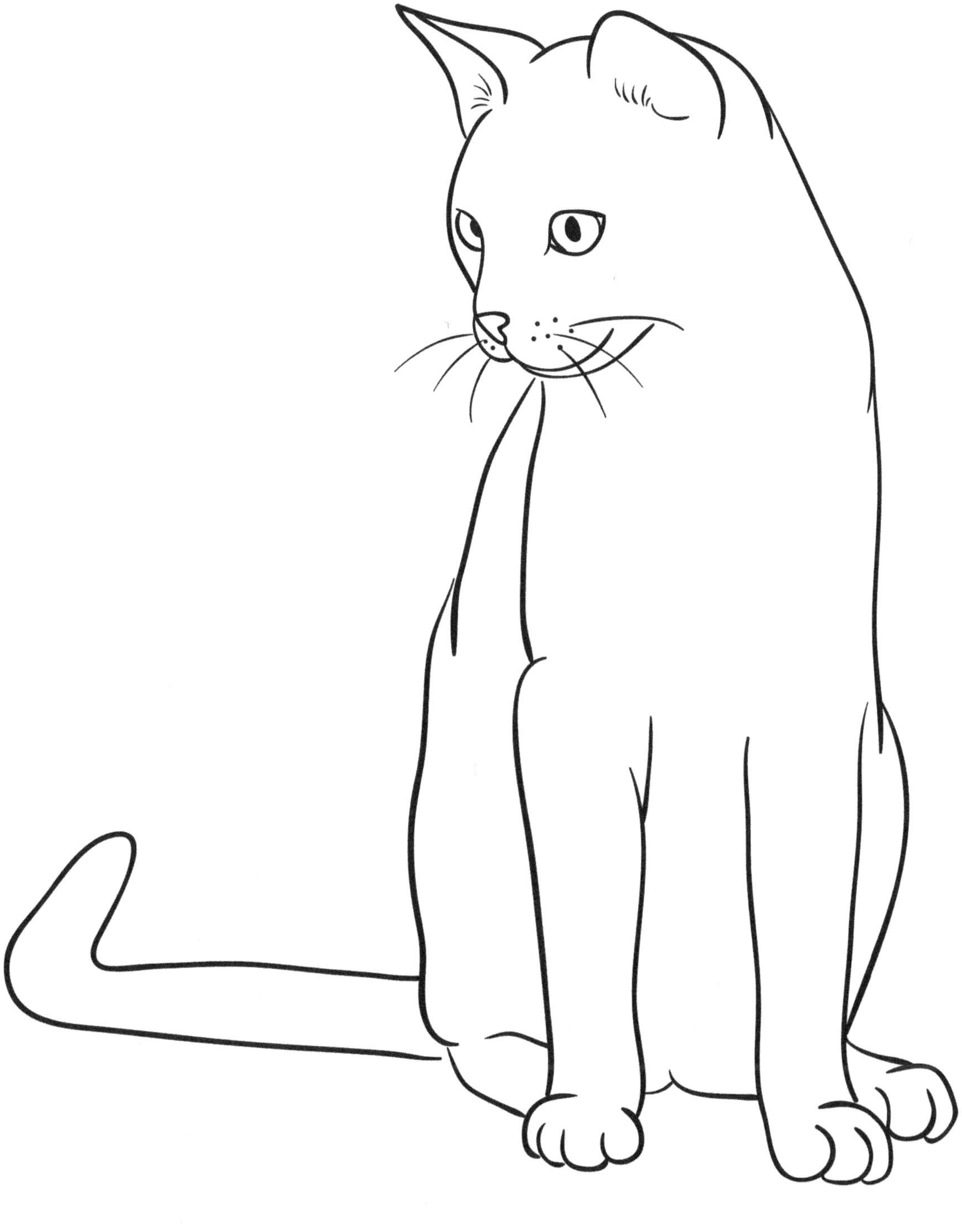

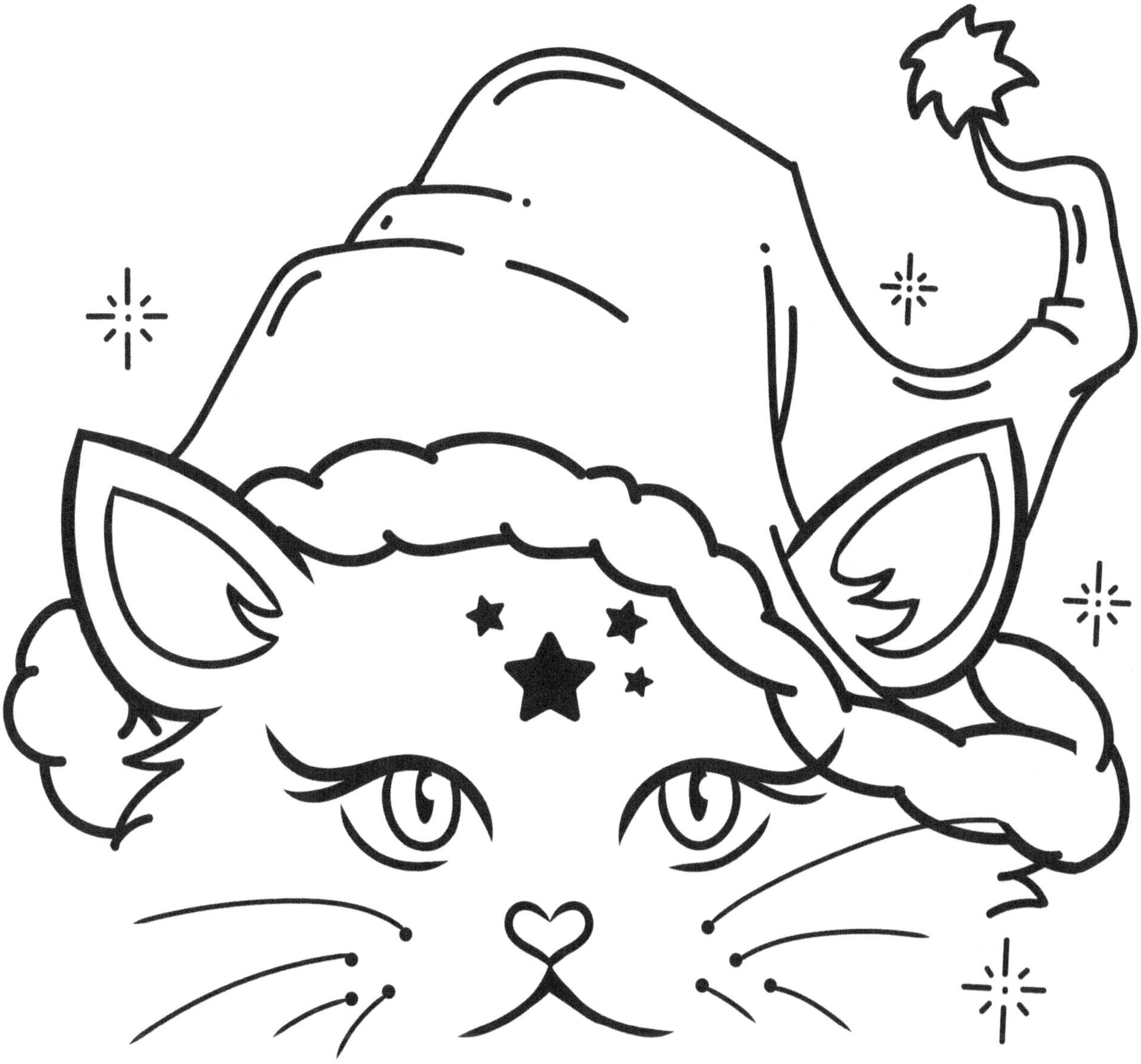

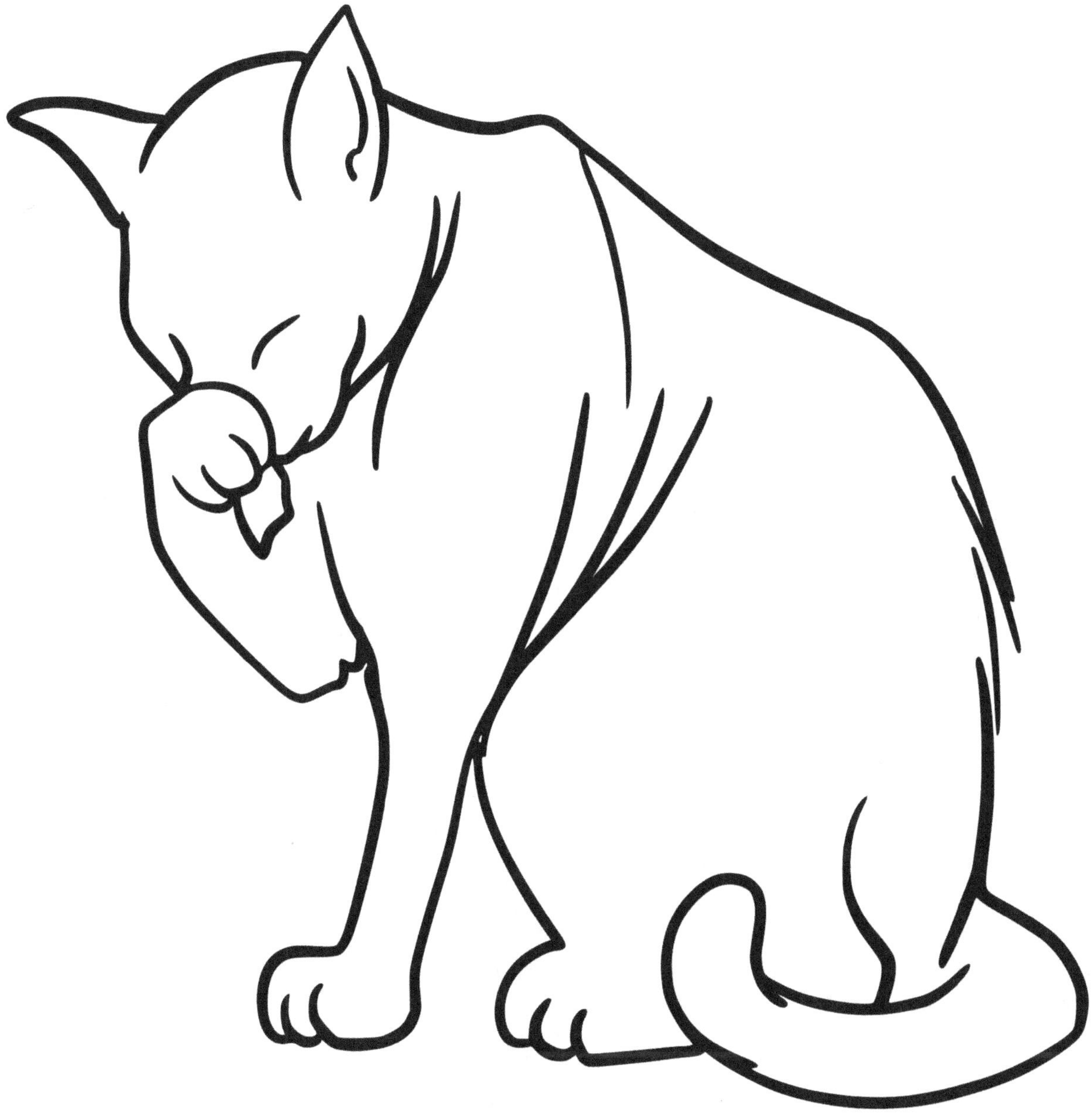

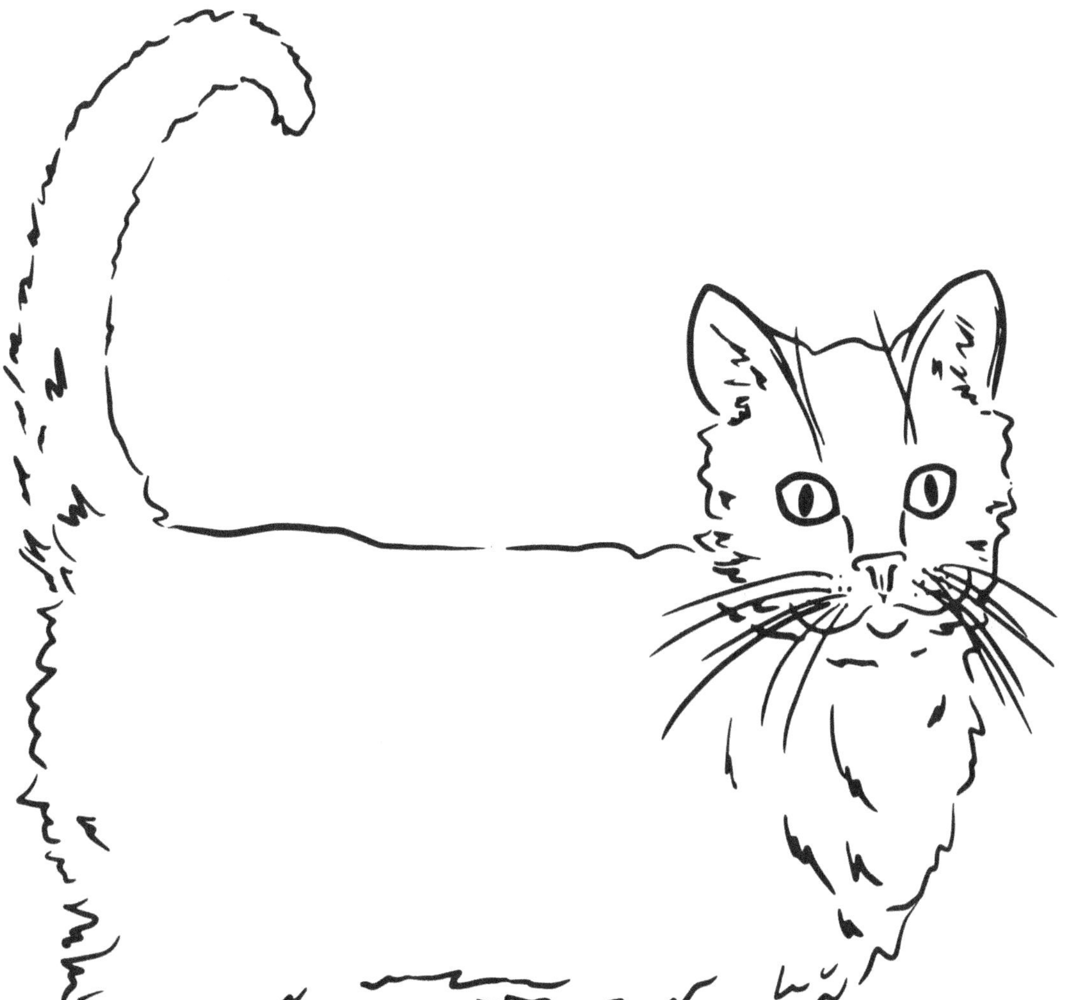

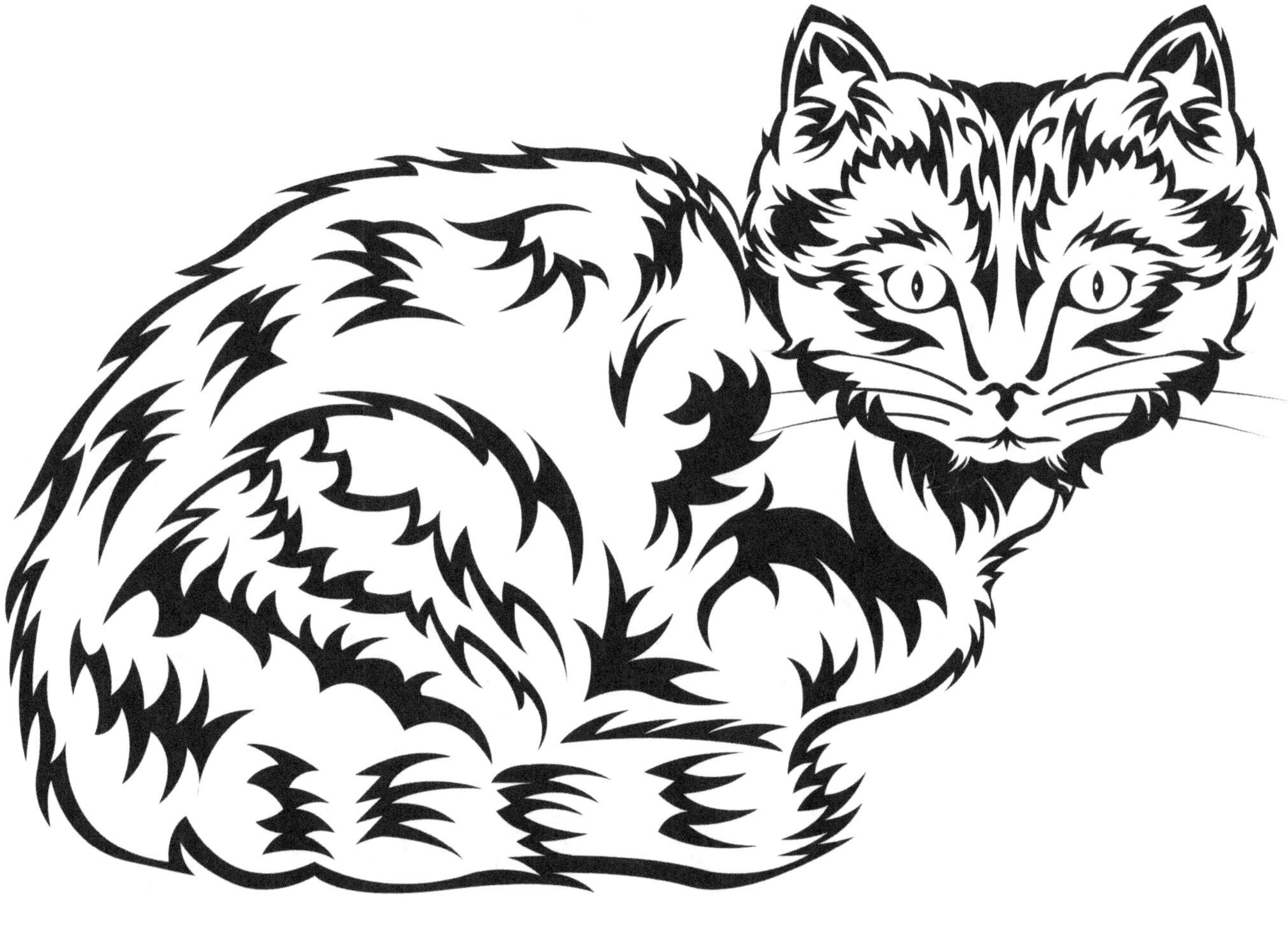

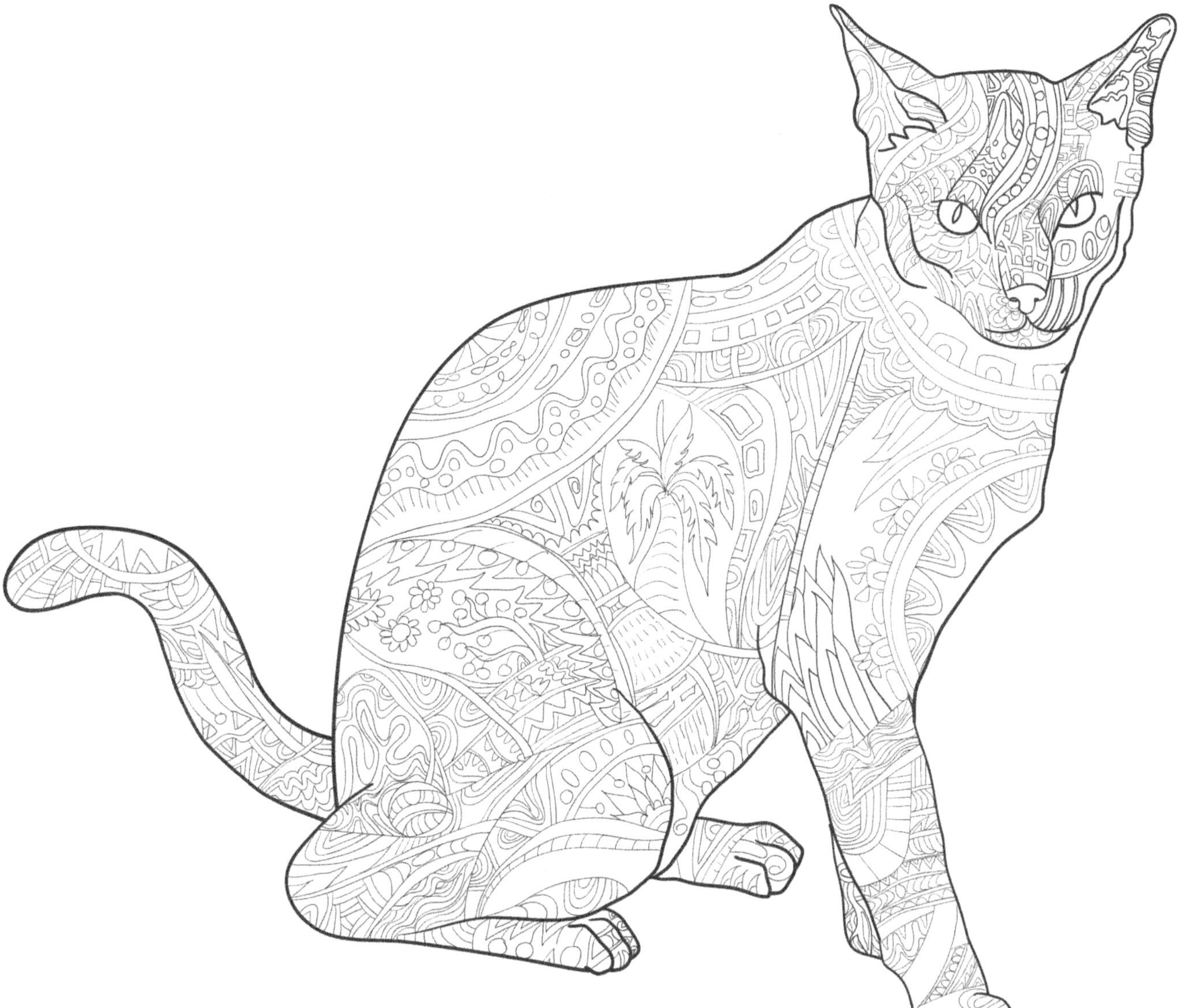

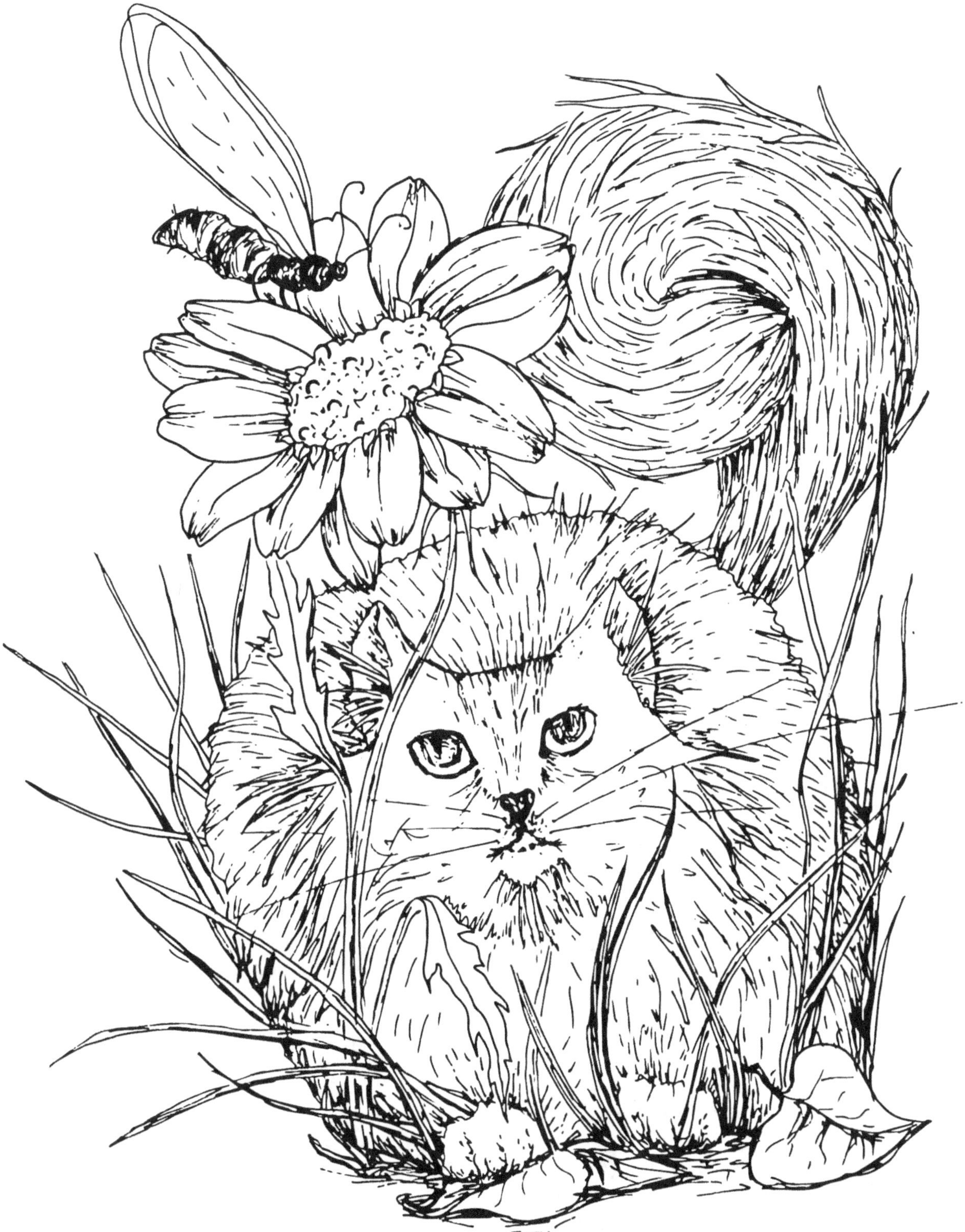

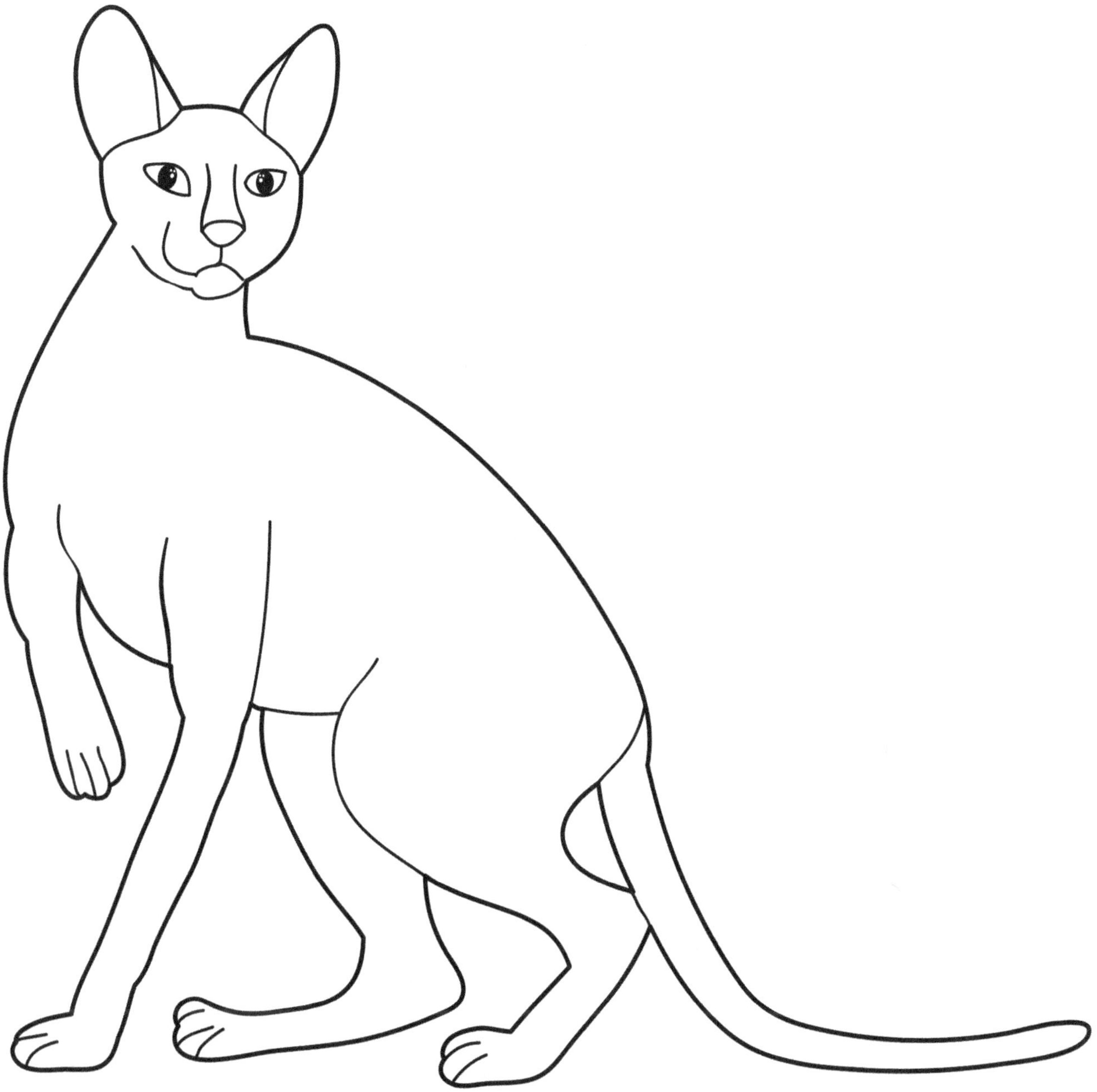

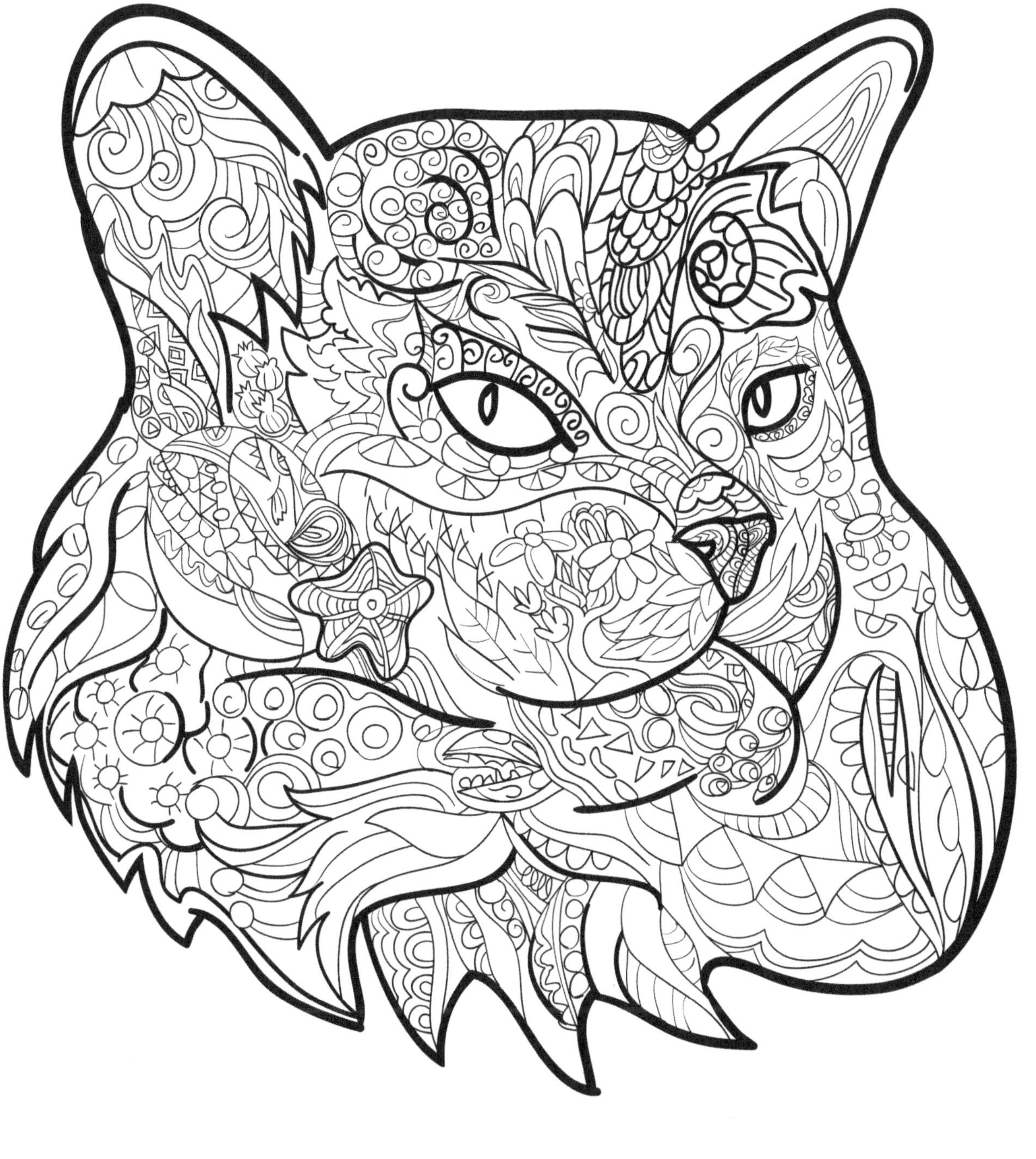

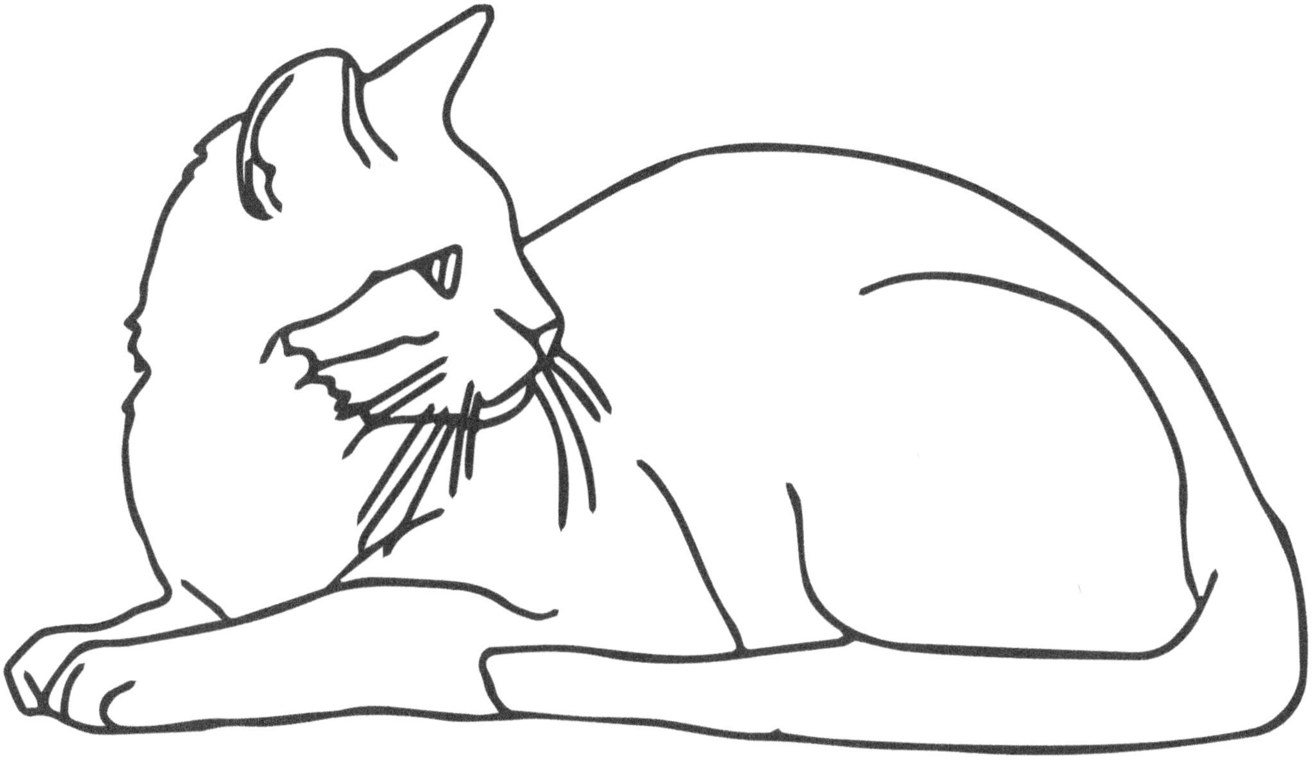

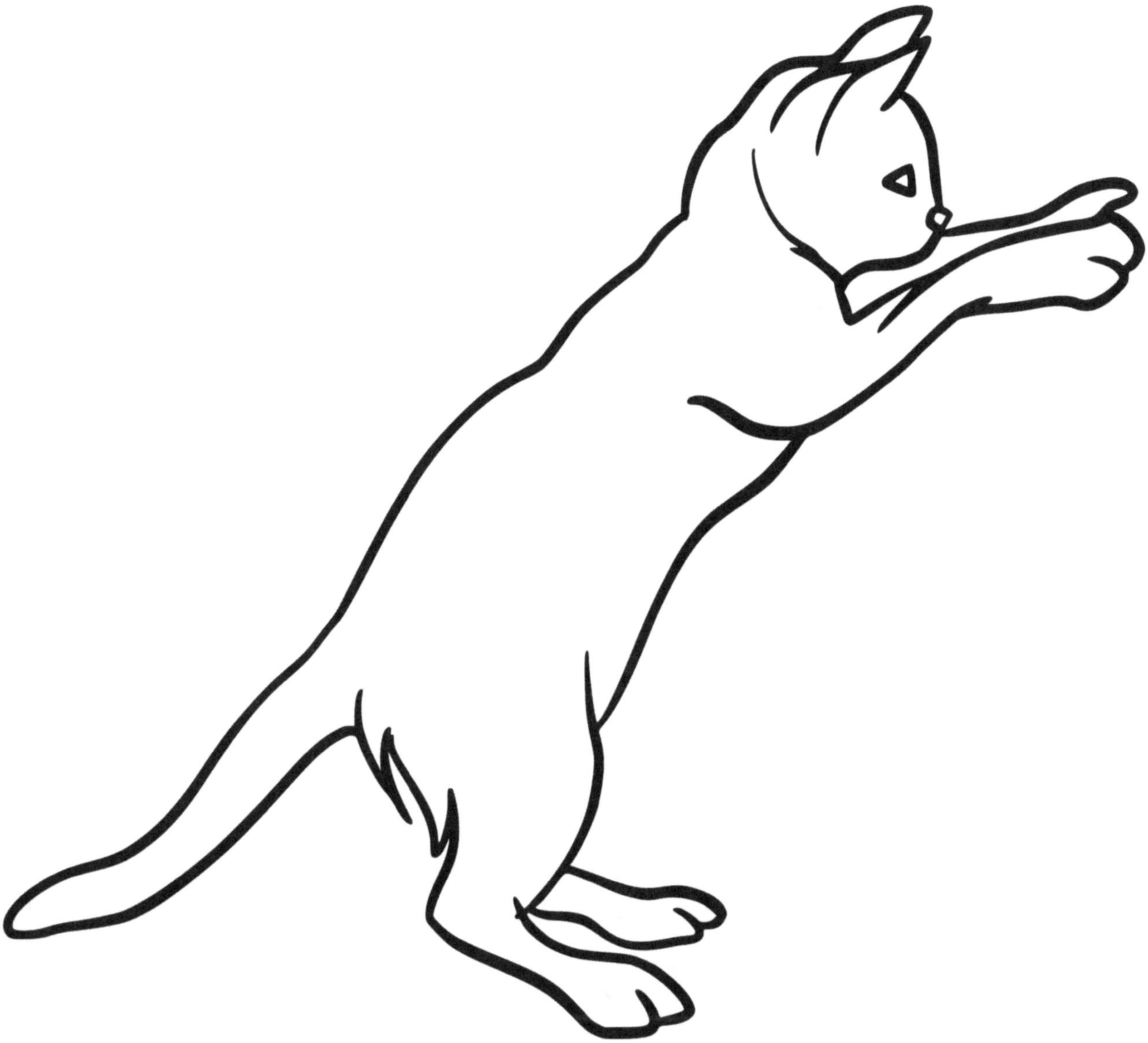

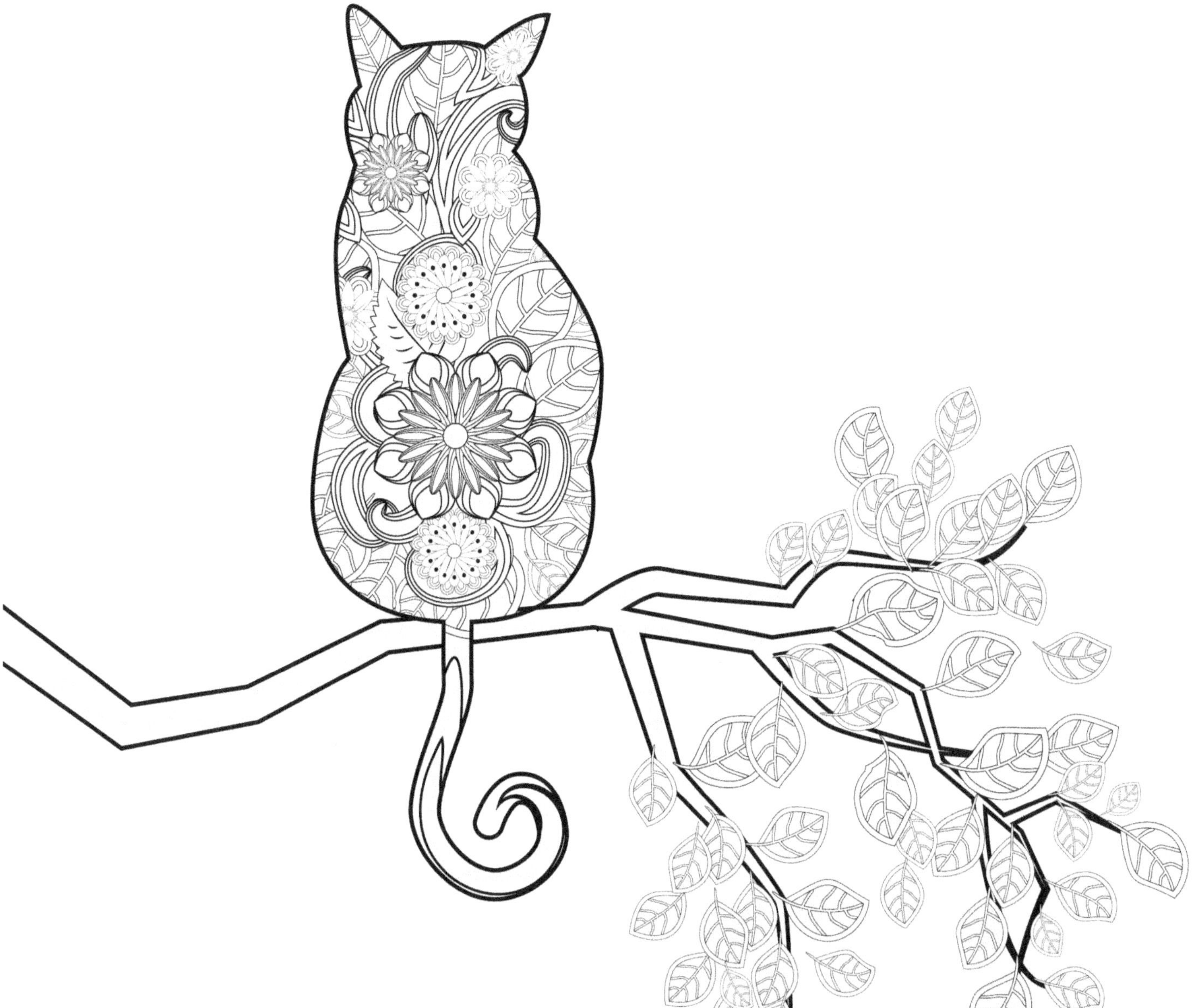

www.ingramcontent.com/pod-product-compliance
Lightning Source LLC
Chambersburg PA
CBHW082150230526
45467CB00043B/2720

* 9 7 9 8 3 7 8 3 1 2 9 5 5 *